Measure Up

by Debbie Mong
illustrated by Diane Paterson

 HOUGHTON MIFFLIN   BOSTON

Printed in China

ISBN 10: 0-618-89865-4
ISBN 13: 978-0-618-89865-7

14 15 16 17 18 0940 20 19 18 17 16

4500590856

Oatmeal Crunchies

1 c warm butter

$\frac{1}{2}$ c white sugar

$\frac{1}{2}$ c brown sugar

1 egg

$1\frac{1}{2}$ c flour

$1\frac{1}{2}$ c oats

$\frac{1}{4}$ tsp salt

1 tsp baking soda

1 tsp vanilla

Combine ingredients. Drop spoonfuls onto pan and bake at 350°F for 10 minutes.

Take the "Measure Up" Challenge:

Can you follow the "Oatmeal Crunchies" recipe with only this measuring spoon and this measuring scoop? If you try the challenge, ask an adult to help you.

Step 1: Cream the butter. That means you stir it with a fork until it is smooth. The recipe calls for 1 cup (c) of butter.

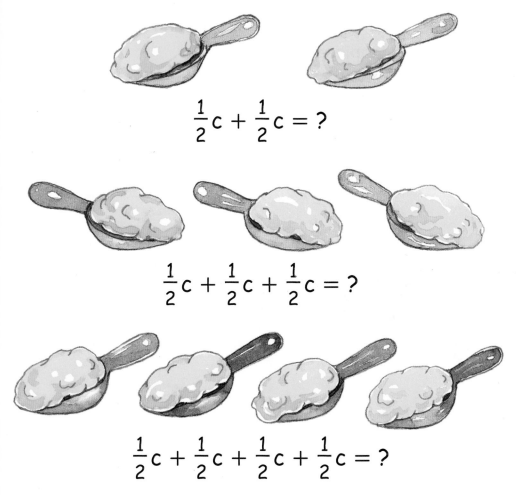

$$\frac{1}{2}c + \frac{1}{2}c = ?$$

$$\frac{1}{2}c + \frac{1}{2}c + \frac{1}{2}c = ?$$

$$\frac{1}{2}c + \frac{1}{2}c + \frac{1}{2}c + \frac{1}{2}c = ?$$

Read·Think·Write The scoop holds $\frac{1}{2}$ cup (c). How many scoops of butter should you use to get 1 cup (c)?

Step 2: Add the sugar. Check the recipe on page 2 to find out how much to add. Mix the butter, the white sugar, and the brown sugar together.

Step 3: Add the egg to the mixture and stir well. Watch out for pieces of shell!

Read·Think·Write How many scoops of white sugar will you need? How many scoops of brown sugar?

Step 4: Add the flour and the oats. You will need $1\frac{1}{2}$ cups (c) of each. Stir well after you add each one. The batter might be a little difficult to stir now.

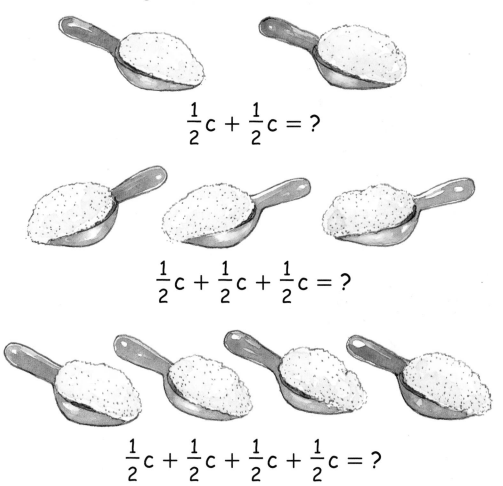

$$\frac{1}{2}c + \frac{1}{2}c = ?$$

$$\frac{1}{2}c + \frac{1}{2}c + \frac{1}{2}c = ?$$

$$\frac{1}{2}c + \frac{1}{2}c + \frac{1}{2}c + \frac{1}{2}c = ?$$

Read·Think·Write How many scoops of oats will you need to make $1\frac{1}{2}$ cups (c)?

Step 5: Use the $\frac{1}{4}$-teaspoon (tsp) measure to add $\frac{1}{4}$ teaspoon (tsp) of salt to the mixture.

Step 6: Add the baking soda and the vanilla. You need 1 teaspoon (tsp) of each.

Mix well. Put small spoonfuls of the batter onto a greased cookie sheet. Use your thumb to flatten each cookie a little. Ask an adult to help you bake the cookies, at 350°F, for 10 minutes.

Read·Think·Write How many $\frac{1}{4}$ teaspoons (tsp) of vanilla should you use to add up to 1 teaspoon?

Now you only have one thing left to measure ...
how many Oatmeal Crunchies you want to eat!

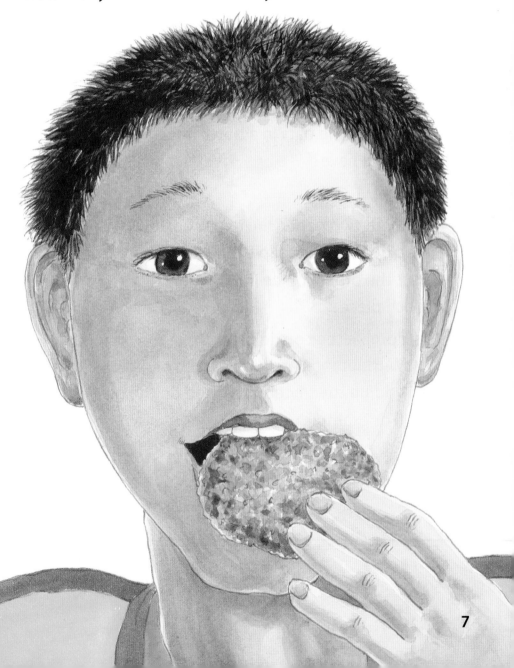

1. **Note Important Details** Add the white sugar plus the brown sugar. How much sugar is there altogether in this recipe?

2. If you put the white sugar, the brown sugar, the flour, and the oats in a bowl, how many cupfuls will you have?

Activity

Cut out two paper circles as cookies. Cut one cookie into 4 equal pieces. Label each piece $\frac{1}{4}$. Cut the other cookie into 2 equal pieces. Label each piece $\frac{1}{2}$.

- Jumble the cookie pieces.
- Without looking, pick up 2, 3, or 4 pieces and add up the fractions written on the pieces. (For example, $\frac{1}{2} + \frac{1}{2} = 1$.)
- Ask a classmate to check your addition by placing the cookie pieces together.